HEALING

Olivia Cooney

Archway Publishing books may be ordered through booksellers or by contacting:

Archway Publishing
1663 Liberty Drive
Bloomington, IN 47403
www.archwaypublishing.com
844-669-3957

Interior Image Credit: Olivia Cooney

ISBN: 978-1-6657-3065-5 (sc)
ISBN: 978-1-6657-3066-2 (e)

Library of Congress Control Number: 2022917621

Print information available on the last page.

Archway Publishing rev. date: 10/27/2022

Contents

The Darkest of Times 1

    Innocence 2

    Women's Equity 3

    Exposed 5

    Witch Hunt 6

    Unseen Marks 8

    Demons 9

    Numb 11

    Rose Colored Glasses 12

    Unraveled 14

    Body and Soul 15

    Wither 16

    Sober 18

    Self-destruction 19

Times of Transition 21

    Perspective 22

    Twisted House 23

    Life Cycle 25

    Death vs Life 26

Uncomfortable Growth 27

Backbone 28

When I Wake 30

Quilting 31

Sleepless Hollow 32

Renewal 33

Rebirth 34

Supernova 36

Tanzanite Dreams 37

Wisteria 39

Sunday Sunrise 40

Daisy 42

Lotus Flower 43

Auntie Kisses 45

Yin and Yang 46

Gray 48

Summer Sunset 49

Christmas Joy 50

Fine Like Wine 51

Afterword 53

About the Author 55

Thank you to my friends and family for their endless support.
And for "Little" Andy who left us too soon…

This book includes mature themes such as mental illness, abuse, sexuality, and politics.

THE
DARKEST
OF TIMES

Innocence

A jack-in-the-box shares my mind.
But its erratic behavior leaves me on edge.
Like a kite battered by the wind, I am the whole of a torn piece.
They say it is my fault for standing too close,
for not closing my eyes as blinding light shot out from a single atom.

Purity, not light, makes one blind.
Virginity drags you to the depths of the abyss and leaves you there with the rotting flesh.
Until all the innocence rots away, you cannot see.
Only once the marrow has degraded, does color begin to reveal itself.

The dark black and blue shades reek of sadness and loneliness
And I wish to vanish from it like Houdini and his jail break.
But leaving this room means being plagued by strawberries and cotton candy.
Forevermore like a jack-in-the-box.

Women's Equity

You say I am too much, but you never stop talking,
even interrupting me.
But that's ok for you to do with your five-o'clock shadow
and chauvinism.
Your expectations of me are "reasonable".
Me: available at your beck and call.
Playing the multiple roles of baggage handler, therapist, and best friend.
My wishes, to be free in a world made for everyone,
troublesome, annoying, immodest.
It is unnecessary for me to want equity in your mind.
Vexatious, even.
If only I was red-blooded like you.
But then that'd make me domineering not assertive,
You take initiative while I can only take a negative tone.
Your mistakes are glossed over while mine are under a microscope
Where does the misogyny end and my rights begin?
Certainly not just in the domestic.
I deserve a say in my health care, in whom I marry, in where I work.
I deserve a choice in how many kids I have, in what books I read and where I get an
education, what I eat, who I sleep with and when.
When did men decide they were the keepers of women?
Where do my rights begin?

Exposed

I am guilty of nothing but existing.
Yet, you hold me down and strip me of my clothes until I'm bare and naked.
Your fancy blue and red suits smell of wealth and power.
"The American Dream."

You fight over whether there should be more red or blue suits.
Or maybe just less pink.
All the while, I am still naked and exposed.
Vulnerable to your every want and need.

And now we must debate whether two pink suits can stand together and hold hands, or if our jewelry should be stripped of us, too.
Your American Dream is to be wealthy and powerful.
Mine is to not be raped by your power.

Witch Hunt

Witches.

They are only what you make of them.

Yet, you start a hunt anyway.

Burn them down!

You chant viciously, as if we've done something wrong.

Witches!

You cry out into the night.

We hide in fear because we have no magic spells to use.

But you insist on pounding down our doors with your pitchforks and torches.

Hunting us like wounded animals.

Screaming utterances of Bitch and Whore at us.

Because we boldly equated ourselves with you, for one lifetime too long.

Olivia Cooney

7

Unseen Marks

Indelible marks across my soul you've left.
Pain and stain bring shame upon me.
Even the cleanest water cannot cleanse me of you.
Your marks are not easily hidden.
Anxiety pounds down on me like a hailstorm.
Nothing drowns it out and I fear I am going mad.
I may suffocate in this pain.
All the while still breathing, still yearning,
for a time when you did not exist.

Demons

I

No matter how much sleep I get, I am chased by demons.

Sleepless, cold entities that chase me until I can no longer

feel my legs.

I break into a cold sweat just to know they are there even if I cannot see them.

They drag me from my bed and tear me to pieces.

Enveloping me in their darkness.

But their kill is quick and soon I wake.

And while I am afraid, being haunted by demons is better than being haunted by you.

II

Being haunted by you is like drowning in quicksand.

Dark, abrasive, and confusing.

Pain-filled lungs cry out in agony but make no sound.

I've lost my voice during this slow, terrifying death.

I have several false awakenings.

Each time getting sucked back down into your depths.

Finally, I awaken and take a breath of fresh air.

Freedom is finally mine.

I go to take my first steps only to realize I am covered in your cement.

Still drowning, even on dry land.

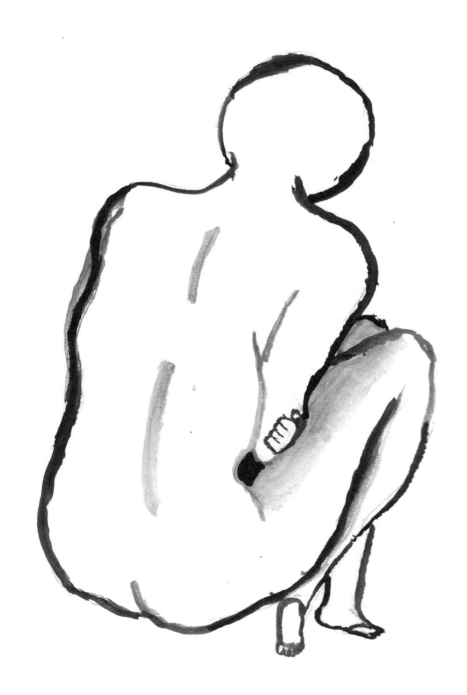

Numb

Roses are red and violets are blue, but I can only see the colors I feel.
And I cannot feel anything.
I feel no warmth or cold.
I do not feel wet or dry.
I only feel numb and stretched into the void.
I *am* the void, a dark abyss.
I am nothingness and numbness, plainness and emptiness.
Even solitude would be something worth feeling but I feel none of that.
I only feel the colors I can see, and I am blind.

Rose Colored Glasses

Greener grass grows on this side, it must be true.
The dew shines bright, but it is a slick slope.
Red sunsets always precede the darkness but are not always seen; especially when we see
in shades of rose.

Hindsight, dark grievances have passed, clouding my judgement and my emotions.
How to escape from something no longer active?

Unraveled

Twisted dark eyes and waves of thunder roll across the sky.
It's raining needles and knives.
There's a sound stuck in my throat, and it sounds like death.
It comes out in screeching notes like a banshee with a wail on her breath.
Sleepless nights and fickle fights plague this uneasy mind.
And like a fine ball of twine, I am unraveled.

Body and Soul

Loneliness is like a bloodstain on the soul.
And the call of the wolves hangs low over the moon.
The wild trees bend shadows into shapes.
Their roots long to dive deeper, soaking in all the emotion of
a love sick teenager.
But the roots are shriveled up and the wine they make tastes bitter and fruitless.
The wind howls with pain as water fills the lungs of this vessel.
Pain is inevitable but survival is not.

Wither

I want to watch you wither like the last leaf on a winter's tree; dry, cold, and lonely.
The bland taste of your love dying over and over. Yesterday, today, but not tomorrow.
There's only room for one of us in my life and if I must choose (and I must) then I choose myself.
No skipped heartbeats of hesitation or leaking eyes.
Just a tall tree shedding its last leaf before the night falls.

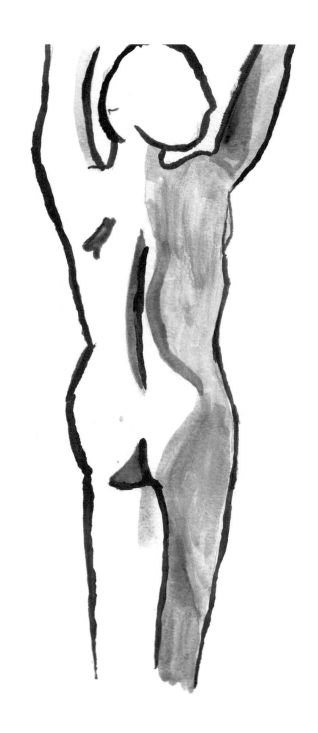

Sober

I used to think we were star-crossed lovers like Romeo and Juliet.
Now I think you just got high off the pain you inflicted.
And maybe I learned to get drunk off the pain of being ripped apart.
Almost three years sober now but your wounds are just as deep.
Only now they are called scars.
As if time cures all.
But time never healed Humpty-Dumpty, and you still plague my memories.
Seven years I was addicted to you.
Maybe it'll take just as long to mend as it did to gather all these wounds.

Self-destruction

Water dripping,
drip, drip, drip.
Water dribbling,
quiet, soft, pitter-patter.
Water flowing,
cool, calm, peaceful.
Water flooding,
rushing, torrid, gushing.
Water rising,
growing, surging, swelling.
Water drowning,
panicking, burning, suffocating.
Water dripping,
drip, drip, drip.

Olivia Cooney

TIMES OF TRANSITION

Perspective

Solitude.
Grey eyes staring with such intensity, and the cold marble sea staring right back.
An icy wind ripping through the coast.
Sand whipping around the legs.
The stony clouds promising rain, pouring down from the sky.
The lonesome whistle of an empty beach.

A quiet morning.
Grey eyes warming to brown.
The sea giving a jolt of excitement.
The warmth of the sun cuts through the chill in the air.
A calm breeze stroking the paleness of skin.
Clouds parting around the sun, giving way to light.
A song of freedom flows down the beach.

Twisted House

A house rests on a quiet street.
Sometimes alive with parties, other times seemingly abandoned
The house sits, none the less.
The street on which it is perched, is full of neighbors but sleepy.

The house is in an ever-changing state of flux.
The living room in mostly just a pass through.
The dining room a place for junk, or things we promise we'll get to… eventually.
The kitchen a place for large parties to gather.
The family room the setting to unwind, and the sunroom stays ever locked.

The stairs creak and groan with the weight of every step.
The hallway brightly lit when in use but pitch black when empty.
Each bedroom a different color.
One, various shades of black.
The room directly across dotted with yellow and purple.
The master, a calming green.

Some days you visit all the rooms, while others just the dark rooms.
Still, other days, you stay up and visit the bright party rooms all night long.
The rooms you visit depend on the pills you take, Alice.
Some make you small, some make you tall.
But the house is always there.
Hosting both the parties and the sleepiness.

24

Life Cycle

A massive thunderstorm and a downed tree.
A log stagnant in the river.
Water rushing by, cold and icy.
The greenest moss growing over top.

Lightning rarely strikes twice, but when it does…
A log floating down the river on a gentle, foggy morning.
The log slick with sweat as it floats with the greatest of ease.

Not lightning this time, but a torrent.
Cascading down the craggy plight.
A log shredded by nature, splintered and diffused.
The river winding into several small streams.
A log shattered from the inside out, drifting down many paths.
Never to be whole again.

Death vs Life

Admire me and pluck me like a rose.
Put me in a vase as a trophy and mind my thorns as you submerge my broken stem in water
until you lose interest and
my petals wither down to the table.

Appreciate me and plant me like a wildflower.
Surround my roots with nutrients allowing me to deepen and spread.
And forget-me-not as I bloom, and you watch me attract the prettiest of butterflies.

Uncomfortable Growth

Chaos is home and peace is unsettling.
Yelling and screaming, fighting for your life.
It's completely natural until it's not.
The silence that follows is uncomfortable but necessary.
It's hard to grow in peace but it's harder to grow in chaos.

Backbone

I ache from standing so tall for so long.
Like a giraffe who is tired of holding their neck above the water and wants to lay down and sleep I am exhausted, but my backbone is a willow, strong and flexible to the winds of change.

When I Wake

I cannot let this trauma go.
The reaper who wants what they did not sow.
All I feel is broken, broken, broken.
You thought I'd forever be your token.
Every night that I lay down to sleep,
all I can ever do is weep.
I'd like to get rid of these nightmares of you.
And while I'm at it, all memories of us too.
But now I know that when I wake,
I'll have better memories to make.

Quilting

I am a quilt patched together.
My dark, broken fragments spliced together by blinding white and yellow.
Quilts are made from broken pieces yet are whole in themselves.
The reason for sewing patches together is more important than the patches alone.
Without reason they are just fragments strewn about and while I have darkness in my past, I am still whole.

Sleepless Hollow

These painful feelings held in the palm of my hand,
in this dreary sleepless hollow, will keep me here until I learn
to let them go.

RENEWAL

Rebirth

Impossible to distinguish one water droplet from another, I drowned in a river of personalities.

Changing to suit what other people needed: a river, a swimming hole, a basin of water at the end of the night.

Until I dried up and all, but one drop of water remained.

Then the rain came, slowly at first, then torrentially.

Now I am a powerful flood washing the previous world away.

Saving two of everything in the Ark.

My own Ark of the Covenant.

Created by flowing water, thick as blood and just as red, too.

The water subsides and Life remains.

But the river is where I come alive now, no longer drowning in another's wake.

Now, I am my own Life Force.

A calm river connecting portraits and sustaining vitality.

Olivia Cooney

Supernova

Tell me about the time you became a supernova;
exploding with color and richness into the abyss.

A pinpoint of light.
Massless, ghostly.
Unfolding into dark thickness.
My undoing in the blackness of light, agonizing over the pain of life, unravelling my unconsciousness into the depths of my soulless body, unbuttoning the fabric of the cosmos.
The darkest reaches of the universe cannot find me. I am willingly
lost and found at the same time.

Tanzanite Dreams

I only asked for diamond dreams, but you said they weren't rare enough.
So, I reimagined my dreams, made them of emeralds and sapphires and rubies.
But still you dismissed them.
Finally, I suggested Tanzanite, one of the rarest dreams to have.
You suggested cubic zirconia, worth less than my diamond dreams, and told me I should be happy without any gemstone dreams.
I finally realized the truth:
you didn't want me to dream bigger.
You didn't want me to dream at all.
So, I left you behind with your worthless dreams made of cubic zirconia and nothingness.
And went and mined my own tanzanite.

Olivia Cooney

Wisteria

Wisteria can only grow where the sun shines full, the soil is good, and it has support.

But you planted me like ivy, and still expected me to bloom on command

My roots breeched your structure, searching for affection, but all I found was empty intimacy.

Still, I reached further in, horrified by what I found.

Your structure was rotting away.

Broken glass and rotting flesh.

And I knew, I too, would wither if I stayed.

So, I stretched my roots out further and found the sun.

I uprooted myself from your structure and planted myself elsewhere.

Sunday Sunrise

The fresh frosting of dew soaks into the grass as dandelion seeds scatter like stars around the universe.
A gentle breeze rocks the meadow and the trees sway to the music
of songbirds and cicadas.
Wildflowers gather in celebration releasing a sweet perfume.
The pink and orange hues of the sunrise dance along the horizon like a
stained glass window.
And the quiet melody of the morning sets a peaceful tone for the day.

Olivia Cooney

41

Daisy

A purple flower in your hand and a smile across your face as you look at the life around you in wonderment.
The gardens of vitality are at your whim and the meaning of life reveals itself in the purple daisy you carry with you.

Lotus Flower

Daydreams of frogs on lily pads, butterflies floating on lotus flowers, dragonflies zooming by, and the peaceful water's lonely cry.
I sit on the edge of the dock whistling a quiet tune as I wait for the soft drizzle of rain to cool off the morning air.

Olivia Cooney

Auntie Kisses

You gently lean your forehead into my face signifying that you want kisses.
Usually, I get an outstretched hand warning me to keep my distance.
But right now, you're leaning forward, giggling warmly, letting me know that today you want auntie kisses.

Yin and Yang

A koi fish swims gracefully in the clear-as-day water.
Shades of orange, black, and white melting together creating beautiful watercolor paintings
in a pond full of hopes and dreams.
Two koi, one midnight black the other sunset orange circle each other
reminding us that two are the same even if they are different.

Olivia Cooney

Gray

The mood strikes so rarely but with wild hair and tame eyes she screams danger and radiates peace.
Robustness fills the atmosphere with the pink and purple hues of a cotton candy sky.
Perfume wafts through the air creating the ease of vanilla and coconut coupled with the tranquility of lavender.

Summer Sunset

Puffy marshmallow clouds drifting by waving away the rain inside for some hot summer sun. Reminders of the yellow starburst remain long after the sun has set in the fields of sunflowers that radiate warmth even on the coolest of nights.

The rush of wind in a butterfly's wings must feel exhilarating like a rollercoaster of fun. Skydiving into the afternoon and landing just as evening dawns on us.

Crickets sing into the setting sun and echo our sweetest dreams as we lay our heads down to sleep.

Christmas Joy

You've fallen asleep wearing your blueberry dress even though it's December.
Tucked very gently into your small hands are your favorite Christmas ornaments from Grandpa's house.
Usually, you cuddle a stuffed animal but tonight, the holiday spirit
has overcome that tiny body with a big soul and filled it with joy.

Fine Like Wine

Life ages you like a fine wine; well-rounded with a bold aftertaste.
Fruity and velvety, yet earthy.
When made well, it goes down like liquid gold and becomes a wine you remember for a lifetime.
The roots of the vine are well aged, and if over fifty, marketed as "old".
Old vines have the distinct down-to-earth taste of wisdom and maturity
and leave the rest of us with a palate for the finer things in life.

Afterword

This collection of poems grew mostly out of experiencing emotional abuse during a long-term relationship and the happiness I found during my healing. I decided to take some time to be by myself for a while after the relationship ended. I chose to do this so I could detangle my thoughts and start healing properly. Detangling these thoughts is a difficult process. It becomes necessary to question everything and even once you find the answers you often second guess them.

Grief is an emotion you experience a lot of during the healing process. Many of these poems deal with grief of some form. Grief of a lost relationship, of years wasted, of my cousin who is no longer with us. It can be overwhelming at times and can throw your day off balance. Trying to date before healing, certain smells, even certain songs were all things that could take me right back to feeling trapped and overwhelmed. I experienced a great deal of anxiety and depression after leaving my situation, but also a great deal of relief.

After grief comes of period of transition. A time when things start to get better slowly. You experience grief intermixed with moments of happiness. You may feel moments of happiness and suddenly grief kicks in again. Or vice versa. I felt guilty for feeling happy, but I also felt like something was wrong with me to still be grieving something that was so unhealthy.

Joy follows the period of transition. This joyful period is when you feel happiest in your journey of healing. There may still be times when your question yourself or moments where grief shows through again, but mostly you feel hope and joy. I found a great deal of hope in my niece and nephews. I became secure in being by myself because I was now secure within myself. I had put myself into therapy to overcome co-dependency and find confidence in myself.

In this collection there are 13 heavy poems, 9 transitional poems, and 13 hopeful poems. Healing is a difficult and sometimes frustrating journey, and I am grateful to myself, my friends, and my family for allowing me to take the time to work on myself. I still have moments where I question if what I experienced was real or if it's all in my head but that's common with emotional abuse. Ultimately, I am still healing but am in a much better place in life than before. I chose to turn my poems into a book in the hope that someone will understand both the pain and the joy experienced during the healing process.

About the Author

Olivia is a Columbus, Ohio native. She enjoys backpacking, spending time with family and friends, researching genealogy, and writing. She began writing poems in high school as a way to cope with stress. She finds inspiration in nature and life experiences.

Printed in the United States
by Baker & Taylor Publisher Services